Born Again

The Whole Story: What Jesus Really Meant

By You Must Be Born Again

BornAgainTruth.com

Scripture quotations are from the
King James Version unless otherwise noted.

Cover and Layout by Michael De Hoyos, Jr.

ISBN (paperback): 979-8-9948635-1-0

Published by Kanan Road Publishing
www.kananroadpublishing.com

Born Again

The Whole Story: What Jesus Really
Meant By You Must Be Born Again

WILLIAM MORAN

KANAN ROAD
PUBLISHING

Table of Contents

Preface: How "Born Again" Lost Its Depth

> *Jesus answered him, "Truly, truly, I say to you, unless one is born again, he cannot see the kingdom of God."*
>
> **- John 3:3**

Have you ever been asked the question, "Have you been born again?," and were not quite sure how to answer it? The phrase "born again" is one of Christianity's most familiar—and misunderstood—expressions. For much of my life I, too, wrestled with its meaning. Raised Catholic, I drifted from faith in my youth and led a life of the flesh, pursuing worldly pleasures, only to be reawakened decades later by an unexpected invitation from a businessman I greatly admired. During a presentation, he encouraged the audience to consider developing their spiritual lives. Without offering details, he invited anyone interested to leave a business card so he could send helpful information. I eagerly did.

Several days later, I received a small pamphlet entitled *Are You Born Again?* It spoke about the need for a relationship with Jesus. After years away, I returned to church and began attending Mass regularly. At the same time, I was listening to television preachers and reading the Bible on my own. Before long, I realized I was hearing two very different answers to the same question. On one hand, I encountered passionate calls to "accept Jesus into my heart," and repeated appeals to "have a personal relationship with Christ." These well-spoken preachers stirred my emotions deeply. I felt awakened from a long spiritual slumber and sincerely grateful for the businessman whose encouragement had started the journey.

Yet confusion soon followed. What I was hearing did not fully align with what I remembered from my Catholic upbringing. Many of the television preachers suggested that I did not need the Church—only the Bible and a private relationship with Jesus. Unsure how to reconcile these voices, I went to confession and told the priest about my recent spiritual awakening. When I asked him how one becomes born again, he smiled warmly and replied, "You already are." He explained that baptism is the moment of new birth, and that the grace given there continues to unfold throughout life. His answer unsettled me—not because it lacked depth, but because it contradicted much of what I had been hearing elsewhere.

I continued attending Mass while listening to the preachers who had first stirred my heart. I loved Christ, but I did not yet understand why His followers seemed to tell such different stories about how new life in Him begins. Reconciling those perspectives—Scripture and experience, emotion and sacrament, personal awakening and the Church's ancient teaching—became a journey that would change not only how I answered the question "Have you been born again?" but how I understood the Christian life itself. This book is the fruit of that journey.

Introduction

One day, someone directed me to watch a YouTube video. The video featured an encounter between Christian evangelist Ray Comfort and a young Catholic girl. The conversation reminded me of that businessman who years earlier helped awaken me, and the pamphlet he would later send me encouraging a personal relationship with Jesus, not with the Church. Ray asked the girl if she had been born again. She replied, a bit unsure, "We don't believe in that," and when he pressed her– "Do you know where that comes from?"– she guessed, "A religion, right?" Ray confidently answered, "No, it's from John chapter 3 in the Bible," and then proceeded to recite the passage.

I had a sense that the girl was right, but I didn't know how the term came to have such significant meaning. Ray began asking the girl whether she had broken any of the Ten Commandments, and when she said, "Sometimes I miss Mass," Ray replied, "That's alright." I thought, huh, one of the commandments is to honor the sabbath, and for Christians, that became Sunday. He seemed sincere and knowledgeable; he could recite Bible verses and had a good way about him, so I wondered why he would respond that way.

I decided to open my Bible and look for the verse Ray quoted, and sure enough, Jesus says, "You must be born again." I was surprised to see that Ray never mentions that, when Nicodemus asks Jesus how a person is born again, Jesus responds plainly: "Truly, truly, I say to you, unless one is born of water and the Spirit, he cannot enter the kingdom of God" (Jn 3:5). Why would a self-proclaimed Christian evangelist omit something so obvious, especially when it is Jesus's own explanation? I agreed with the young girl in the video, thinking that "born again" was a religion or denomination, but I did not know its origins. This curiosity led me into a deeper study—into Scripture, the early Christians, Church history, and the origins of the modern born-again movement. I wanted to know where this newer interpretation came from, how it developed, and why it differs so sharply from what Christians had believed for nearly two millennia.

What I discovered was that Ray's omission was not accidental; it reflected an entire modern worldview in which "born again" is severed from what Jesus really meant. That brief exchange stirred something in me. I began to wonder how a phrase so plainly explained and understood for years could be presented so differently and with such confidence.

What I came to discover was that Ray was right: being born again does come from the Bible. However, he and other evangelists teach a particular way of being born again that is not how Jesus intended. While the kind of spiritual awakening they offer is valuable, it is not the whole story. In the earliest centuries of Christianity, being born again was not something you declared—it was something God *did* to you through His Church.

So how did a phrase that once pointed unmistakably to baptism become a defining slogan of modern Evangelicalism? To answer that, we must trace the long journey from the sacramental life of the ancient Church to the revival tents of the eighteenth century, through the preachers and publications of the early twentieth century, and finally into the religious vocabulary of our own day.

This is the story of how the new birth, the mystery of water and Spirit, was gradually transformed into a slogan of modern Christianity. This book seeks to recover the depth, coherence, and beauty of the original Christian vision. Chapter 1 begins by exploring the biblical and historical foundations of being "born again," as understood by Christ, the apostles, and the early Church. Chapter 2 traces the shift that emerged through the revivalist movements of the eighteenth and nineteenth centuries, when conversion increasingly became framed as an interior crisis rather than a sacramental beginning. Chapter 3 examines the early twentieth century and the influence of *The Fundamentals*, where this new understanding of regeneration was codified in writing and given doctrinal boundaries. Chapter 4 moves into the mid-twentieth century, showing how mass media, celebrity preachers, and cultural forces further reshaped the language of new birth. Chapters 5 and 6 conclude the narrative by considering the cumulative effect of this evolution. They examine how a phrase once rooted in sacrament and Church came, for many, to function as something resembling a new religion altogether, much like the young woman in the video who instinctively identified "born again" not as a belief, but as a category of its own.

My hope is that by rediscovering the whole story, readers will come to see the Christian life not as a single moment to be remembered, but as a lifelong adventure of grace—an ongoing transformation and a real participation in the very life of God.

Chapter 1

The Original Meaning: Born of Water and Spirit

Before "born again" became a slogan, a testimony, or a cultural identifier, it was a mystery spoken by Christ Himself. When Jesus told Nicodemus that one must be "born of water and the Spirit" to enter the kingdom of God, He was not inviting speculation or emotional interpretation; He was revealing how new life in God actually begins. The earliest Christians did not debate what this meant. They baptized. They understood the new birth not as a feeling to be chased or a decision to be announced, but as a divine act. It was God's work, accomplished through water, Spirit, and faith within the life of the Church. When Nicodemus approached Jesus at night, he came as a scholar and a seeker. "Rabbi," he said, "we know that you are a teacher come from God: for no man can do these miracles that thou doest, except God be with

1

him" (Jn 3:2). Jesus's reply must have startled him: "Truly, truly, I say to you, unless one is born again, he cannot see the kingdom of God" (3:3). Nicodemus, confused, asked, "How can a man be born when he is old?" (3:4). Jesus answered with the verse that defines Christian initiation: "Unless one is born of water and the Spirit, he cannot enter the kingdom of God" (3:5).

The Greek word translated "again" is *anōthen*, which also means "from above." Jesus was not calling for a second natural birth, but for a spiritual birth that comes from above, from God himself. These were not abstract poetic words. Jesus was drawing on a pattern that had been present in Scripture from the very beginning, a pattern that every Jewish teacher should have recognized. Former Baptist and Catholic apologist Steve Ray notes: "God always starts new things in the same way—with 'water and the Spirit.'"[1] And indeed, from Genesis to Jesus's own baptism, this pattern is unmistakably clear.

The Old Testament Backdrop

Water and Spirit are the birthplace of the new creation, as described in Genesis 1:1-2. The Bible

---

1 Steve Ray, "Are You Born Again by 'Water and the Spirit'?," *Defenders of the Catholic Faith (CatholicConvert.com)*, n.d., https://catholicconvert.com/further-thoughts-on-water-and-the-spirit/.

opens with water covering the deep and the Spirit of God hovering over the waters. Creation itself is born through water and Spirit: the primordial image of God bringing forth life. The vital nature of these two elements is revealed again and again in the Old Testament.

The Flood (Gn 6-9)

The Jews often called Noah "the second Adam" because God was beginning again. Once again:

- Water cleanses the earth

- The dove (symbol of the Spirit) hovers over the waters

- St. Peter explicitly connects Noah's rescue to baptism: "Baptism ... now saves you" (1 Pt 3:21)

The Exodus (Ex 14)

Israel's birth as a nation happens through:

- Passing through the parted waters of the Red Sea

- Guided by the pillar of cloud and fire—images of the Holy Spirit

- St. Paul describes the Exodus as a kind of baptism (1 Cor 10:1-2)

3

When Jesus spoke to Nicodemus, the Jewish people were already familiar with the symbolism of water and Spirit. He was revealing the fulfillment of ancient prophecies. This wasn't a new idea—it was the fulfillment of everything Israel had been waiting for. When Jesus told Nicodemus about being born of water and Spirit, He was pointing directly to these prophecies:

The Prophets (Ezek 36:25-27, Is 44:3)

Israel was promised a new covenant defined by:

- Clean water
- A new Spirit within
- A new heart enabling obedience

Christ's Actions and Words

Christ Himself established baptism at the heart of the Christian life through both command and example. He explicitly instructed His apostles to baptize all nations, thereby instituting the sacrament as a universal mandate for entry into discipleship (Mt 28:19). Though sinless, Jesus nevertheless submitted to John's baptism, identifying Himself with sinners and revealing the path of obedience through which humanity is brought into the will of God and opened to new life. He further promised that salvation would be joined to both faith and baptism, declaring, "He who believes and is baptized will be saved" (Mk 16:16).

He explained to Nicodemus that entrance into the kingdom requires being "born of water and the Spirit" (Jn 3:5). Taken together, Christ's words and actions leave little doubt that baptism is not a human invention but a divinely instituted means by which God grants new birth and saving grace.

Saving grace is the free and unmerited gift by which God draws the human person into communion with Himself and makes eternal life possible. It is not merely God's favor or a feeling of assurance, but a supernatural participation in the life of God, bestowed entirely by His initiative. Through saving grace, the soul is forgiven, restored, and elevated beyond its natural capacities, enabling it to believe, hope, and love in a way ordered toward salvation. This grace originates in Christ's redemptive work and is ordinarily communicated through the sacraments, beginning with baptism, which brings about spiritual rebirth and justification.

Saving grace does not coerce the human will or guarantee perseverance apart from cooperation; instead, it empowers freedom, calling the believer into a lifelong response of faith, repentance, and obedience. In this way, salvation is neither self-generated nor mechanically imposed, but a living relationship initiated by God and sustained by His grace until its fulfillment in glory.

St. Paul teaches that salvation itself is the work of grace: "By grace you have been saved through faith; and this is not your own doing, it is the gift of God" (Eph 2:8). Grace is not opposed to human weakness but given precisely because of it; God tells Paul, "My grace is sufficient for you, for my power is made perfect in weakness" (2 Cor 12:9). Scripture presents grace not merely as pardon, but as a transforming power that changes the believer from within. "The grace of God has appeared … training us to renounce ungodliness and worldly passions, and to live self-controlled, upright, and godly lives" (Ti 2:11–12).

Grace also has an interior, sanctifying dimension: believers are "justified by his grace" (Rom 3:24) and made "partakers of the divine nature" (2 Pt 1:4). Even perseverance is attributed to grace, not self-confidence: "By the grace of God I am what I am, and his grace toward me was not in vain: but I laboured more abundantly than they all: yet not I, but the grace of God which was with me." (1 Cor 15:10). From beginning to end, Scripture testifies that grace is God's active presence working in the soul—initiating salvation, sustaining faith, empowering obedience, and bringing the believer to completion.

The Early Church and Baptismal Rebirth

From the earliest centuries to modern times, Christians understood exactly what Jesus meant when he said, "You must be born again." It is the sacrament of baptism. The Fathers of the Church consistently saw John 3:5, the verse often omitted, as the scriptural foundation for the sacrament that makes a person a new creation:

> **Justin Martyr (second century)** wrote: "We have learned from the apostles this reason for baptism … that we may obtain in the water the remission of sins and a new birth." (*First Apology* 61) [2]

> **Irenaeus of Lyons (second century)** was a disciple of Polycarp, who was a disciple of St. John. Irenaeus taught that through baptism, "we receive the Spirit of God and are made new." (*Against Heresies* III.17.1) [3]

> **Tertullian (second century)** said plainly: "No one can attain salvation without baptism; especially because the Lord says, 'Unless a man be born of water and the Spirit,

---

2   Justin Martyr, *First Apology* 61, The Ante-Nicene Fathers, vol. 1, ed. Alexander Roberts and James Donaldson (Hendrickson, 1994), 183
3   Irenaeus of Lyons, *Against Heresies* 3.17.1, in ibid., 441.

he cannot enter the kingdom of God.'" (On Baptism 12) [4]

Augustine (fourth century) called baptism "the visible word"—the outward act that accomplishes what it signifies: "The sacrament of baptism is the visible form of invisible grace." (*Tractates on the Gospel of John* 80) [5]

Through the centuries, these early writers saw baptism not as an empty ritual but as a divine mystery—the point where the human soul was cleansed, reborn, and filled with the Holy Spirit. To be "born again" was to die and rise with Christ, as Paul wrote: "We were buried therefore with him by baptism into death ... so that we too might walk in newness of life" (Rom 6:4).

Water, Spirit, and the Womb of the Church

The early Christians often described baptism as the "womb" of the Church, where believers are born into new life. The catechumens (those preparing for baptism) were seen as unborn children of faith,

---

4   Tertullian, *On Baptism* 12, The Ante-Nicene Fathers, vol. 3, ed. Alexander Roberts and James Donaldson (Hendrickson, 1994), 674.

5   Augustine, *Tractates on the Gospel of John* 80.3, Nicene and Post-Nicene Fathers, First Series, vol. 7, ed. Philip Schaff (Hendrickson, 1994), 344.

awaiting their rebirth at the Easter Vigil when they would descend into the water and emerge as sons and daughters of God.

In this view, being "born again" was never understood as a single emotional moment but as the beginning of a lifelong journey into the life of God. Baptism stood at the starting line, not the finish line. As Ludwig Ott explains, "Baptism is that sacrament in which man being washed with water in the name of the Three Divine Persons is spiritually reborn." In baptism, sanctifying grace, which Ott calls "a supernatural state of being which is infused by God and permanently inheres in the soul," is poured into the person, cleansing them from sin, incorporating them into Christ, and enabling them to live by faith, hope, and love.[6]

The New Testament Biblical Pattern

The New Testament consistently ties new birth to baptism. Each passage explicitly links rebirth to baptism and echoes the same truth found in the Old Testament, that God uses visible water and invisible Spirit together to bring new life.

- **Titus 3:5:** "He saved us … by the washing of regeneration and renewal of the Holy Spirit."

6 Ludwig Ott, "Doctrine of Baptism" and "Doctrine of Sanctifying Grace," in *Fundamentals of Catholic Dogma*, trans. Patrick Lynch (TAN Books, 1974).

- **1 Peter 3:21:** "Baptism … now saves you."

- **Acts 2:38:** Peter's response to "What must we do?" is "Repent and be baptized for the forgiveness of sins."

- **Acts 22:16:** Paul's conversion, where Ananias tells Paul: "Arise, be baptized, and wash away your sins."

- **Ephesians 5:26:** Christ sanctifies the Church "by the washing of water with the word."

Jesus's Own Baptism: The Pattern Revealed Before Nicodemus Arrives

Before Jesus speaks with Nicodemus, He undergoes His own baptism in the Jordan:

- He descends into water

- The Spirit descends upon Him

- The Father declares Him the beloved Son

Water. Spirit. Sonship. Immediately after this event, John's Gospel tells us Nicodemus comes to Jesus with questions about new birth. The timing is not accidental. Every Jew in Jerusalem had heard about Jesus's baptism; it was "the news of the week." As Steve Ray observes, Jesus's explanation of "water and Spirit" applies to Nicodemus what had already been revealed in his own baptism.

God consistently uses water and Spirit as the birthplace of new creation, and Jesus Himself defined the new birth as rebirth through water and Spirit. The early Church lived this truth. Unmoored from its biblical roots (the apostolic teaching that Christ promised would be guided by the Holy Spirit until the end), a powerful cultural and theological movement began to take shape. A movement that would change the Gospel's understanding of rebirth and set the stage for a dramatic shift in how Christians spoke about and experienced being "born again."

In the next chapter, we will look at how the Great Awakening, born from sincere zeal and noble intentions, gradually redefined the new birth. What had always been safeguarded within the Church as a mystery of grace, rooted in water and Spirit, and handed down through apostolic tradition, slowly came to be recast as a sudden moment of emotional crisis.

Chapter 2

Revivalism and the "New Birth Experience"

Before we explore the revivalism movement of the eighteenth century, in which the "born again" movement emerged, it is worth spending a few words on what preceded it. The divergent views of baptism held by Luther, Calvin, and Zwingli unfolded alongside the very movements they founded, forming a trajectory that would shape Protestant Christianity for centuries.

Martin Luther (1483–1546), whose protest began in 1517 and led to the formation of Lutheranism across Germany and Scandinavia, retained a strongly sacramental understanding of baptism. For Luther, baptism truly conveyed forgiveness of sins and incorporation into Christ, received through faith in God's promise.

Ulrich Zwingli (1484–1531), who launched the Swiss Reformation in Zurich in 1519, decisively moved away from this sacramental realism. In defending infant baptism against the Anabaptists, he reframed it primarily as a covenantal sign marking inclusion in the Christian community, explicitly denying that the water itself conveyed regenerating grace.

John Calvin (1509–64), whose *Institutes of the Christian Religion* appeared in 1536 and whose reforms in Geneva during the 1540s gave lasting shape to the Reformed and Presbyterian traditions, occupied a middle position. Calvin described baptism as the "sign of initiation" by which believers are received into the Church and engrafted into Christ, yet he carefully distinguished the outward sign from the inward work of the Spirit, resisting any notion that the rite itself automatically conferred grace.

Taken together, these developments reveal a clear arc: from Luther's baptismal realism, to Calvin's covenantal "sign and seal," to Zwingli's primarily symbolic initiation. As sacramental causality receded and interior faith was increasingly emphasized, the language of new birth became progressively detached from baptism, preparing the theological ground for later revivalist preaching that would relocate regeneration almost entirely into a personal, emotional conversion experience.

This theological arc did not remain confined to sixteenth-century debates; it reshaped the Christian imagination in ways that would bear fruit centuries later. As baptism was gradually reinterpreted as a sign that primarily expressed faith rather than a sacrament that objectively conferred grace, the locus of spiritual certainty shifted inward. Assurance was no longer grounded principally in God's action through the Church's sacraments but in the believer's interior experience of faith. Preachers could now speak of conversion as a decisive inner crisis rather than an ecclesial initiation, because the sacramental framework that once anchored regeneration had been loosened.

This shift produced understandable passion—but also profound confusion. It unintentionally replaced Jesus's explanation of new birth with a modern one. Before we can understand how this happened, we must first understand the foundation. Only then can we examine the revivalists, the tent meetings, the anxious bench, *The Fundamentals*, and the men who helped redefine the meaning of being born again.

With the sacramental framework already weakened and assurance increasingly sought within the individual, the eighteenth century was primed for revival, and the Christian world was changing. Across the American colonies and parts of Europe, a wave of preaching known as the Great Awakening began stirring souls and shaking traditions. Men like Jonathan Edwards and George Whitefield set out to awaken a sleepy, complacent Christianity. Their goal was perhaps noble: to call men and women to repentance, to rekindle faith in Christ, and to make religion deeply personal. But something unexpected happened.

Edwards and Whitefield did not create this inward turn; they inherited it. What they did was give it unprecedented force, scale, and emotional intensity. In their preaching, the question of salvation became urgent and personal, pressing hearers toward an immediate reckoning with God. Conversion was framed less as entry into the Church through baptism and more as an unmistakable inner awakening, a moment when one knew, felt, and experienced the reality of grace. The Great Awakening thus marks the point at which a centuries-long theological shift broke into popular consciousness, transforming regeneration from a sacramental beginning into a dramatic experience to be sought, remembered, and proclaimed.

Jonathan Edwards (1703-58) approached revival as a theologian and philosopher. Deeply influenced by Reformed theology, Edwards insisted that true conversion involved a genuine inward transformation of the affections, understood as a supernatural work of grace that reordered the loves of the soul. He was cautious, even skeptical, about purely emotional displays. Tears, trembling, or enthusiasm, he warned, were not reliable signs of regeneration. In works such as *Religious Affections*, Edwards sought to distinguish authentic spiritual renewal from mere psychological excitement. Yet even in his careful theology, the new birth was increasingly framed as an interior experience discerned by inward signs rather than as a sacramental act received through baptism. Assurance shifted toward the individual's ability to identify evidence of grace within the soul.

George Whitefield (1714–70), by contrast, was a preacher of extraordinary emotional power. Crossing the Atlantic repeatedly, he carried revivalism to massive crowds in Britain and the American colonies, preaching outdoors with urgency and dramatic intensity. Whitefield's sermons centered relentlessly on the need to be "born again," a phrase he thundered with such force that it became synonymous with Evangelical conversion itself. Unlike Edwards, Whitefield placed little emphasis on theological analysis and much focus on immediate response. His preaching pressed listeners toward a moment of decision, a felt encounter with grace that could be named, dated, and testified to publicly. In White-field's hands, the language of new birth was no longer primarily theological—it was experiential, memorable, and portable.

Together, Edwards and Whitefield represent two complementary paths within the Great Awakening. Edwards gave revivalism its theological justification; Whitefield gave it its emotional momentum. Both, however, contributed to the same outcome: regeneration is increasingly understood as an inward crisis rather than a sacramental beginning. What had once been anchored in baptism was now sought in experience, setting the pattern that later Evangelical movements would inherit, amplify, and normalize.

In their desire to make faith simple and urgently personal, the revivalists gradually shifted the meaning of the new birth from something God does to something the individual feels. The ancient Church understood rebirth as a sacramental reality, a participation in Christ's life through the grace given in baptism, nourished through the Eucharist, and strengthened through a life of discipleship. To the ancients, the new birth was *objective*, *tangible*, and *transformative*. It was not dependent on one's feelings but on God's action.

The Great Awakening began to recast this mystery as an emotional crisis, a dramatic inward experience that proved one's salvation. Sincerity and intensity became the measure of spiritual authenticity. Tears, trembling, and a burst of religious fervor were taken as signs of the Holy Spirit's work. And in time, many equated salvation itself with the feeling of being saved.

The danger was subtle but profound: people began confusing emotional experience with actual grace. Instead of a lifelong process of transformation into Christ rooted in repentance, sacrament, and discipline, many believers were taught to rely on a single moment of passion.

The results were powerful, sincere, and often spiritually fruitful. But they also marked the beginning of a profound shift: a movement away from the Church's continuous teaching on rebirth that would forever change how millions understood the Gospel, the Church, and the meaning of being "born again."

From Sacrament to Sentiment

This shift was not malicious. Edwards and Whitefield were responding to what they saw: lifeless religion, cold formalism, and churches filled with unconverted members. Their passion was to awaken faith—to make it personal again. But in their reaction to spiritual apathy, they overcorrected. In their hands, the new birth became an interior event, something that could be dated and remembered—"the moment I accepted Christ." While authentic spiritual experiences do happen, this new emphasis subtly transformed Christianity from a *sacramental faith* into a *psychological event*. Faith became less about *being incorporated into Christ's body* and more about *feeling personally assured of salvation*.

The Rise of Conversionism

Historians call this shift conversionism—the belief that the true mark of Christianity is a conscious, identifiable "conversion experience." By the late eighteenth and early nineteenth centuries, this view had spread through America's revivals and camp meetings. People were asked to stand, walk forward, or declare publicly the moment they were "saved."

The "anxious bench," the forerunner to the modern altar call, was born. The "**anxious bench**" (often called the *anxious seat* or *mourner's bench*) originated in early 19th-century American revivalism, especially during the **Second Great Awakening** under preachers like Charles Grandison Finney. It referred to a front pew where individuals publicly sat while wrestling with conviction of sin and seeking conversion—symbolizing a moment of intense inner struggle and decision to repent and commit their lives to Christ.

The Church's ancient language of baptismal regeneration was gradually replaced by a new vocabulary: "accepting Jesus," "inviting Christ into your heart," and "getting saved." For centuries, the Church had said, *You are born again through baptism*. Now it says, "You are born again when you decide to be."

A Mixed Legacy

It would be unfair to dismiss the revivalists outright. They reignited faith in a spiritually weary age. Their preaching produced charity, moral reform, and missionary zeal. But revivalism also introduced a theological confusion that persists to this day—a belief that salvation is achieved through personal decision rather than divine action. In the words of Church historian Jaroslav Pelikan: "The Reformation taught that we are saved by faith alone, but the revival taught that we are saved by feeling alone." [7]

---

7   Jaroslav Pelikan, *The Christian Tradition: A History of the Development of Doctrine*, vol. 4, *Reformation of Church and Dogma (1300–1700)* (University of Chicago Press, 1984), 245.

The Seeds of Evangelicalism

By the end of the eighteenth century, these ideas had laid the groundwork for Evangelicalism, a movement that would define Christianity in the English-speaking world. Evangelicalism retained much of the emotional fervor of revivalism but systematized it into a theology centered on individual conversion. Salvation became "personal," faith became "private," and the Church became optional. The phrase "born again"—once the doorway into sacramental life—was now the password to a religious identity.

In the next chapter, we'll see how this movement took institutional form through *The Fundamentals: A Testimony to the Truth*. This series of essays not only defined early twentieth-century Evangelicalism but also solidified the separation between the biblical "born of water and Spirit" and the modern "born-again experience."

Chapter 3

The Fundamentals and the Fragmentation

By the early 1900s, Protestant revivalism had matured into a distinct religious culture. The emotional conversions of the Great Awakening had hardened into doctrinal statements, and a new movement arose to defend what its leaders called "the fundamentals of the faith." The publication *The Fundamentals: A Testimony to the Truth* (1910–15) became a watershed moment. Financed by two wealthy California oilmen, Lyman and Milton Stewart, the twelve-volume series was written as a coordinated defense of "orthodox" Protestant Christianity against what its sponsors and authors saw as a rising wave of modernism—especially liberal theology and "higher criticism," that is, historical-critical approaches to Scripture that questioned traditional authorship, miracles, prophecy, and biblical inerrancy.

Yet buried within its pages was a quiet but profound theological revision: the redefinition of regeneration, the new birth, not as a sacramental act of grace but as a psychological or moral change initiated by faith alone—a stark departure from the one, holy, catholic, and apostolic faith handed on by Christ.

From Mystery to Mechanism

Two chapters in particular played a decisive role in reshaping how regeneration was explained in early twentieth-century Protestant thought. In volume 10 of *The Fundamentals*—chapter 3, "The Nature of Regeneration," by Thomas Boston, and Chapter 4, "Regeneration-Conversion-Reformation," by George W. Lasher, both authors set out to clarify how a person becomes a Christian. Boston, for example, warns of "false conceptions in grace … mistaking some partial changes … for this great and thorough change," defining true regeneration as a change whereby one "gets not only a new head … but a new heart, to love and embrace it in the whole of his conversation." [8] Lasher similarly critiques contemporary approaches that "emphasize the act of conversion … while regeneration is either ignored, or minimized to nothingness," arguing that

---

8 Thomas Boston, "The Nature of Regeneration," in *The Fundamentals: A Testimony to the Truth*, vol. 10, ed. R. A. Torrey (Testimony Publishing Company, 1910), 29.

Jesus's teaching "in the other Gospels ... involves a new birth, without which it is impossible to meet Divine requirements." [9]

Both authors cite Jesus's command to Nicodemus—"You must be born again" (Jn 3:7)—yet neither engages Jesus's fuller explanation two verses earlier: "Unless one is born of water and the Spirit, he cannot enter the kingdom of God" (Jn 3:5). In isolating the calling to be "born again" from Christ's own description of how new life occurs, the discussion subtly reframes regeneration as a predominantly inward intellectual or moral change, rather than the sacramental and Spirit-empowered rebirth rooted in water and Spirit that Scripture and the early Church uniformly taught. This omission was astounding considering the scope of the work that the authors undertook.

The Fundamentals was supposed to be a statement concerning the fundamentals of Christianity. Since being born again was always considered to be a sacrament, this omission could not have been accidental; it was theological and deliberate. It reflected the broader Protestant tendency, particularly in post-Reformation and revivalist thought, to strip the sacraments of their supernatural efficacy and to interpret all saving acts as interior, psycho-

---

9   George W. Lasher, "Regeneration–Conversion–Reformation," in ibid., 33.

logical experiences rather than outward, incarnational mysteries.

Both men wrote within a Reformed and Evangelical tradition that had long rejected the Catholic (universal) and historic understanding of baptismal regeneration—the belief that God actually imparts new life through baptism. To them, salvation was received by faith alone, through a personal act of repentance and trust in Christ.

If they had included verse 5, they would have had to address Jesus's explicit link between *new birth* and *water*—which the early Church universally understood as baptism. Instead, they isolated verse 7 ("You must be born again") to support their redefinition of regeneration as a purely spiritual, non-sacramental event.

By skipping that line, they detached regeneration from baptism altogether. The "new birth" became an interior moral awakening, a shift of the will achieved by intellectual assent to Christ's lordship and repentance from sin. Grace was reduced to divine approval, not divine participation.

The Logic of Modern Evangelicalism

In many ways, *The Fundamentals* completed what the revivalists had begun. If Whitefield and Edwards relocated the new birth from the font to the heart, *The Fundamentals* systematized it. Their reasoning followed a consistent pattern: salvation is by faith alone, and faith is an act of the individual conscience. Therefore, regeneration occurs the moment one believes.

This redefinition gave rise to what would later be called "decision theology." Evangelists now asked, "Have you accepted Jesus Christ as your personal Savior?"—a question unknown to Christians of the first eighteen centuries.

Fragmentation: Faith Without Form

Once regeneration was detached from baptism, it could no longer be anchored to the Church itself. The visible community of faith became optional; authority and sacrament gave way to personality and preference. Every believer, in theory, could start anew anywhere. Denominational boundaries blurred as the experience of being "born again" became the one unifying badge of authentic Christianity.

But unity built on personal experience cannot hold for long. Without a shared sacrament or ecclesial structure, Christianity continued to fragment. Each new preacher, convinced that his interpretation of the new birth was most "biblical," founded his own movement, denomination, or mission society.

The faith once described by Paul as "one Lord, one faith, one baptism" (Eph 4:5) was now expressed in a thousand competing voices—each claiming to represent the same "born-again" Gospel.

The Consequences for Christian Identity

The cultural effects were dramatic. By the mid-twentieth century, to call oneself a "born-again Christian" no longer meant being a baptized member of Christ's body—it meant having had an experience. The language shifted from *ontological* (a fundamental change in being) to *emotional* (a change in feeling). This shift prepared the soil for the next great wave of American evangelism, which would take the revivalists' message global and stamp "born again" on the vocabulary of modern faith.

A Turning Point in Theology

Looking back, we can see *The Fundamentals* as both preservation and loss. Its authors defended the deity of Christ, the authority of Scripture, and the historic resurrection—but in doing so, they quietly surrendered the sacramental realism that had anchored Christianity since the beginning. The new birth was no longer a *mystery to be received*, but a *formula to be followed*. Faith, once communal and incarnational, became individualized and disembodied.

And yet, even in this fragmentation, a hunger remained—the same hunger Nicodemus felt when he came to Jesus at night. People still longed to be truly reborn, to start again, to have new life flow into their weary souls. The problem was not the desire for rebirth; it was the loss of understanding how God had provided it.

The irony of *The Fundamentals* becomes evident when seen in its broader historical context. Many of the authors and supporters associated with the project were deeply critical of the Catholic Church for being "institutional," "dogmatic," or committed to an authoritative Magisterium. Yet *The Fundamentals* itself sought to accomplish a similar task: to define the essential doctrines of Christianity, to draw boundaries of orthodoxy, and to establish a unified theological identity for Protestants confronting modernism. In rejecting the Church's historic teaching authority, the movement inadvertently created a new authority of its own, one not rooted in apostolic succession but in a self-selected body of writers whose interpretations would become, for millions of believers, the functional equivalent of dogma.

Strictly speaking, *The Fundamentals* was written in response to modernist theology rather than to denominational fragmentation. Yet the two realities cannot be meaningfully separated. Once Protestantism rejected a binding teaching authority, doctrinal unity could only be maintained by consensus—and consensus had already collapsed. Liberal theology flourished precisely because there was no mechanism to resolve doctrinal disputes definitively. *The Fundamentals* thus functioned as an emergency attempt to stabilize belief in a fragmented Protestant landscape, defining "essentials" in a tradition that no longer possessed a universally recognized authority to define them. What it sought to preserve was not merely orthodoxy, but coherence itself.

In the next chapter, we'll see how a well-known Christian preacher, an infamous political advisor, and the president of the United States helped to propel the modern "born again" simplified message to the world stage—cementing the cultural identity of born-again Christianity while, perhaps unintentionally, obscuring the fuller, sacramental story that Jesus told in John 3:5.

Chapter 4

The Rise of Evangelical Language: From Graham to Colson

By the mid-twentieth century, revivalism had evolved from the passionate outbursts of the Great Awakening into a more polished, media-savvy movement. The United States was emerging from the trauma of the Great Depression and two world wars, and in this climate of uncertainty and moral fatigue, the cry "You must be born again!" found fresh power. Evangelists now spoke not only from tents and pulpits but through microphones, radio broadcasts, stadium rallies, and eventually television. Conversion was increasingly presented as an urgent decision that could be made at a particular moment, often publicly identified and remembered.

At the same time, the religious landscape was shifting. Many Protestant churches were becoming

culturally assimilated and, in some cases, less insti-
tutionally cohesive, while Catholic parishes were
expanding rapidly in the postwar suburban boom
through immigration, large families, and strong
sacramental life. Against this backdrop, revivalist
language moved further away from incorporation
into Christ through the Church's sacramental life
and toward the individual's interior experience. The
"new birth" came to be understood less as a lifelong
mystery of grace unfolding through baptism and
discipleship and more as a dramatic turning point—
marked by urgency, decision, and personal assurance—shaping how many Christians came to define
being "born again."

Billy Graham and the Language of Decision

The preacher best known for carrying that cry
into living rooms across America was Billy Graham.
With a clear, consistent, and emotionally compel-
ling message, Graham was filling stadiums. Night
after night, thousands would stream down from
the bleachers in what became known as the *altar
call*—a visible, public act of surrender to Christ. This
moment, which earlier revivalists had called the
"new birth," became the centerpiece of Graham's
ministry. And much like George Whitefield, Graham
was a gifted speaker, known for the same refrain.

At about the same time, other evangelists were preaching a closely related message of personal conversion and "coming to Christ." Oral Roberts emerged in the late 1940s as a healing evangelist, later becoming one of the first major televangelists. His ministry combined altar-call conversion with Pentecostal themes of faith healing and, eventually, prosperity teaching. Rex Humbard became the first preacher to host a weekly televised church service, beginning in 1952; by 1980, his program was airing on hundreds of stations worldwide, blending music, testimonies, and an invitation to accept Christ. In the 1970s, Robert Schuller's *Hour of Power* brought a softer, "positive thinking" version of the same basic appeal, personal faith in Jesus as the key to a changed life, to millions of viewers each week.

Alongside these figures, later voices such as Jerry Falwell and Pat Robertson added a more overtly political edge. Still, they operated within the same Evangelical framework of individual new birth, personal decision, and a direct relationship with Jesus as Savior. Taken together, these ministries helped to ensure that Graham's basic message was not an isolated phenomenon but part of a much broader movement.

Through crusades, radio, and especially television, they normalized the idea that to be a Christian is to remember the night you were "born again"

33

and began a "personal relationship with Jesus"—language detached mainly from the sacramental and ecclesial context in which earlier Christians had understood new birth. This resonated deeply with postwar America, where institutions were mistrusted and individual choice was sacred.

The "Born Again" Identity

As Graham became a national figure, *born again* became shorthand for a dramatic, personal turning point—a moment of surrender in which one accepted Christ and was assured of salvation. By the 1970s, the term had become so culturally recognizable that even secular media adopted it as a label for Evangelical identity. Two figures accelerated this shift. First was Jimmy Carter, whose 1976 presidential campaign marked the first time a major political figure openly described himself as a "born-again Christian." The national press struggled to define the term, and in doing so brought it into mainstream political vocabulary.

What had once been revivalist language became, almost overnight, a sociological category—a way to name a type of believer, a moral outlook, even a voting bloc. By the late twentieth century, sociologists were using "born again" as a demographic label. Polls measured how many "born-again Christians" voted a certain way, supported specific causes, or held certain beliefs. The language of rebirth had become political, cultural, even commercial. What began as the mystery of divine regeneration was now a marker of identity.

The second was Charles Colson, whose 1976 autobiography *Born Again* gave the phrase dramatic visibility. Colson, a former Nixon aide embroiled in the Watergate scandal, narrated his fall, repentance, and spiritual awakening with gripping honesty. His story humanized the phrase and made it synonymous with inner crisis followed by moral transformation. Yet it also reinforced a distinctly modern interpretation of new birth: a deeply personal experience of psychological renewal rather than incorporation into the sacramental life of the Church.

By the close of the decade, *born again* had become a cultural identity and a badge of belonging within the Evangelical movement—a label one claimed, a story one told, a moment one remembered. What centuries of theological drift had begun, late-twentieth-century American culture completed: the migration of new birth from the font to the feelings, from a sacrament to a slogan.

Personal Relationship?

By this time, even the language of "accepting Jesus" or "inviting Christ into your heart" had

35

become standard Evangelical vocabulary. What began as metaphorical expressions in revival preaching were now treated as biblical formulas— shorthand instructions for entering the Christian life. Increasingly, salvation was described not as incorporation into Christ through baptism but as the establishment of a personal relationship with Jesus, a phrase unknown to the early Church and absent from Scripture.

Its rise marked yet another stage in the same trajectory: the relocation of Christianity from the communal, sacramental life of the Church into the interior experience of the individual believer. What the born-again label accomplished for identity, the personal relationship language accomplished for spirituality—shifting the center of gravity from God's action in the soul to one's own private decision and emotional encounter.

The contrast with historic Christianity is striking. The early Church did not speak of "inviting Jesus into your heart" or forming a "personal relationship" with Him in the modern, individualized sense. Its vocabulary was richer, more communal, and profoundly sacramental. As we saw in chapter 1, the New Testament describes salvation not as a private arrangement between the individual and Christ but as incorporation into His Body—a real, ontological union accomplished by water, Spirit, and faith.

St. Paul's language is unmistakably corporate and embodied:

- "For in one Spirit we were all baptized into one body" (1 Cor 12:13)

- "All of us who have been baptized into Christ Jesus were baptized into His death" (Rom 6:3)

- "As many of you as were baptized into Christ have put on Christ" (Gal 3:27)

This is not the language of private spirituality but of participation, of being grafted into Christ's life, death, and resurrection through baptism: and the earliest Christians understood these passages exactly this way. When the Fathers wrote of salvation, they spoke of *rebirth, illumination, the seal, the bath of regeneration, the laver of new life*. They emphasized transformation through the Church's sacraments, not a solitary decision of the heart.

By contrast, the modern phrase "personal relationship with Jesus" shifts the entire center of gravity. It frames salvation primarily as something inward and psychological—a feeling, a moment of decision, a private bond between the believer and Christ. While personal intimacy with God is certainly part of the Christian life, this emphasis obscures the biblical pattern in which God acts first, through visible means, within a visible community.

In other words, the ancient Church spoke the language of incorporation, communion, and rebirth; the modern Evangelical world speaks the language of decision, invitation, and relationship. One is grounded in sacramental and ecclesial belonging, the other in personal experience and interior authenticity. Both seek Christ, but they do so upon the basis of profoundly different assumptions about how grace is given and how the Christian life begins.

This linguistic shift did more than change vocabulary—it reshaped the imagination of millions of believers. It taught them to look inward for assurance rather than outward to the sacramental life Christ instituted. It replaced "How has God united me to Christ?" with "Have I truly meant it?" What baptism had once proclaimed—God's action—the language of personal decision quietly relocated to the human heart. And with that shift, the meaning of "new birth" itself underwent a transformation that the early Church would not have recognized.

Cultural Christianity and the Loss of Mystery

The success of this modern messaging was undeniable. Millions came to faith, and many experienced genuine conversions. But there was an unintended consequence: the collapse of mystery into method. The new birth became something one could schedule—a prayer to be repeated at the end of a sermon. Salvation was packaged into steps. One, admit you are a sinner; two, profess belief in Jesus; and three, confess Him publicly.

While sincere, this formula reflected the modern age's desire for efficiency and control, even over spiritual matters. The mystical reality of grace, of dying and rising with Christ through baptism, of receiving the Spirit in the sacraments, of belonging to His mystical Body, was replaced with the language of *decision, crisis, and personal assurance*.

From Faith as Communion to Faith as Choice

This shift had enormous theological and psychological consequences. Christianity, once communal and incarnational, became individualized and cerebral. The Church had become optional, something nice to attend but not needed, and the sacraments became mere symbols, and faith became a *feeling*.

The very phrase "born again," which once described an objective transformation, now described a subjective experience. The center of gravity moved from *Christ's action in us* to *our action toward Him*. And yet, the universal human desire behind the phrase remained the same—the longing to start over, to be made new, to have life from above. The tragedy is not that Evangelicals speak of being born again, but that the phrase has been narrowed to mean less than what Jesus meant.

The Irony of Evangelical Success

In the process, the sacred had become social. The theological had become tribal. And yet, behind the noise, the truth remains unchanged: the invitation of Christ still echoes—not to an emotional moment, but to a new creation. "Unless one is born of water and Spirit ..."

Chapter 5

When "Born Again" Becomes a Religion

In the modern era, preachers and teachers across denominations have built entire ministries around this single phrase, often detaching it from the whole mystery of baptism, grace, and ecclesial life that Jesus and the early Church proclaimed. In modern usage, "born again" often functions less as a precise theological claim and more as a recognizable identity label—so much so that Pew Research Center uses self-identification as "born again or Evangelical" as a classification tool when denominational identity is unclear. [10]

When the young girl answered, "It's a religion, right?" she was not wrong. For many modern evangelists like Ray Comfort, being "born again" is not

---

10 Pew Research Center, *Religious Landscape Study* (Pew Research Center, 2014), https://www.pewresearch.org/religion/religious-landscape-study/.

just one aspect of the Christian journey—it *is* the entire journey. The term is treated as a theological endpoint rather than the beginning of new life in Christ. Comfort is not alone in this change. Many others within conservative Evangelicalism have contributed to this mindset, each in their own way.

Their passion for personal conversion is sincere, but their message often implies that those who are "truly born again" belong to a higher spiritual class, a kind of spiritual elite whose authenticity is proven by emotional fervor, behavioral perfection, or unwavering assurance. Over time, "born again" ceased to carry the meaning Jesus intended when speaking to Nicodemus. Instead, it became short-hand for a personal, inward experience of salvation, a moment of repentance and belief that allegedly settles one's eternal destiny.

The Problem with "Soundly Saved"

Ray Comfort's ministry, Living Waters, and his book, *The Way of the Master*, have reached millions through videos, street preaching, and evangelism training materials. His message emphasizes sin, guilt, repentance, and the need for personal salvation—all essential elements of the Gospel. However, his teaching on what it means to be "born again" reveals a serious theological problem. On his website (Livingwaters.com), Comfort distinguishes between what he calls "true and false conversion." He writes: "This is going to sound a little radical, but if someone is soundly saved, he will never fall away."[11]

In other words, according to Comfort, if a person ever "falls away" or sins grievously after professing to be born again, it proves that their conversion was not genuine—they were *never truly saved* to begin with. This doctrine, often called "Soundly Saved Theology" or the "Perseverance of the Saints," assumes that true believers cannot ever lose their salvation. While this idea has roots in Reformed theology, Comfort's version takes it to an extreme in psychology. It creates an impossible standard: if you sin after conversion, your rebirth was false. The result? Endless spiritual insecurity. Believers constantly question whether their salvation "took."

The Trap of Perfectionism

This teaching subtly replaces the grace of God with moral performance. Grace transforms, elevates, and empowers, but it never eliminates human freedom. And because we remain free, we remain capable of sinning. Instead of a life lived in

---

11 Ray Comfort, *The Way of the Master* (Living Waters, 2006), and his "True and False Conversion," posted Aug. 9, 2019, https://www.livingwaters.com/true-and-false-conversion/.

communion with Christ, the "born-again" believer is left with a haunting question: "If I stumble, does that mean I was never truly born again?"

The New Testament paints a very different picture. The early Church was filled with repentant sinners—not flawless saints who never failed, but people continually being renewed by grace. Peter denied Christ three times. Paul confessed that he still struggled with sin (Rom 7). The historic Christian view understands salvation as a relationship, not a status. You can fall away and be restored. You can sin and be forgiven. You can fail and still be loved. To be born again does not mean to be *finished*; it means to *begin*. Baptism places divine life in the soul; it does not erase human frailty. Salvation is therefore not a one-time event but a lifelong cooperation with grace, a journey in which weakness becomes the place where God's strength is made perfect. This is why the Church speaks of ongoing conversion, spiritual combat, growth in virtue, and continual renewal of the mind.

Work Out Your Salvation in Fear and Trembling

St. Paul details the New Testament picture beautifully. When he exhorts believers to "work out your salvation in fear and trembling" (Phil 2:12), he is not contradicting grace; he is describing how grace works. This verse often confuses modern Christians because of how salvation has been redefined. In much of contemporary Evangelical thinking, salvation is seen as a completed event—something achieved the moment a person "accepts Christ." But Paul, like the entire early Church, understood salvation as a living relationship, not a finished transaction.

The Greek verb *katergazesthe*, translated "work out," means to bring to completion or carry to its intended end. It implies that salvation is something received in baptism and then cultivated through a life of cooperation with grace. It's not *earned* by works, but *realized* through obedience, perseverance, and sanctification.

The phrase "in fear and trembling" doesn't mean dread or anxiety. It means a profound reverence for the mystery of what God is doing within us. The believer is not cowering before God but standing in awe that divine life has been entrusted to human weakness. Paul continues in the following verse: "For it is God who works in you, both to will and to work for His good pleasure" (Phil 2:13).

That line resolves any misunderstanding. We "work out" what God works in. Grace is the cause; our cooperation is the effect. The Christian life, then, is a partnership in which divine power is expressed through human faithfulness. This passage speaks directly against the idea that salvation is a one-time emotional moment. To be "born again" is to begin a journey, not to finish one. The new birth is *planted* at baptism, but it must be *worked out* in daily fidelity—through repentance, charity, and perseverance.

The "fear and trembling" Paul speaks of is the opposite of the casual assurance often promoted in modern revivalist preaching. The early Church took salvation seriously because it understood its sacramental depth. Grace is a gift, but it is a living gift—one that must be received continually, guarded carefully, and allowed to grow. In this sense, "work out your salvation" is not a rejection of grace but a call to live intentionally in grace. It reminds us that being "born again" is not the end of conversion but its ongoing expression.

When Faith Becomes Self-Surveillance

For many sincere Christians raised in Evangelical theology, life becomes a cycle of profession and doubt, conversion, and reconversion. Instead of resting in the mercy of Christ, they become auditors of their own faith—measuring it, analyzing it, and fearing its insufficiency. Sadly, this is not the freedom of the Gospel. The Christian life is neither self-scrutiny nor a closed system of "true versus false conversion," but self-surrender and an open invitation to continual renewal. The early Church never asked, "Was my conversion authentic?" It asked, "Am I walking with Christ today?"

As Lutheran theologian Chad Bird argues, Christianity is not grounded in a self-defined "personal relationship with Jesus," but in Christ's objective action toward us through His Word, sacraments, and Church—realities that exist whether or not the believer feels spiritually successful. Bird argues that the popular Evangelical framing of Christianity as a private, individualized "personal relationship with Jesus" is theologically misleading because it treats faith as something detachable from the Church and her concrete life. In contrast with Bird's view, Ray Comfort explicitly divides "true and false conversion," insisting that if someone is "soundly saved," "he will never fall away." Bird's critique exposes how "relationship" language can quietly shift Christian assurance away from Christ's objective gifts (Word, sacraments, and communion) toward subjective self-assessment—precisely the instability that conversion-slogans often intensify.[12]

The Loss of the Sacramental Vision

For nearly two thousand years, John 3:3 was understood as the beginning of the Christian life—the moment when a person was born again through baptism, receiving divine life through water

---

12 Chad Bird, *Upside-Down Spirituality*, chap. 8, 159–76.

and Spirit. Every ancient Christian, every Church Father, every early catechism recognized this as the moment of rebirth. A rebirth that was not merely emotional, psychological, or symbolic—it was a sacramental reality, the work of God acting through visible signs.

By reducing "born again" to a self-contained experience, modern preachers have inadvertently removed the Church from the process of salvation. In the original Christian vision, rebirth was both spiritual and physical, an event in time and a mystery beyond time. It occurred in baptism, through water and Spirit, within the Church, the Body of Christ. When the Church's sacramental role is stripped away, the believer is left alone, isolated from the visible means of grace and forced to find assurance within personal feelings and behavior. That isolation is precisely what Christ came to end. He founded a Church so that rebirth would never depend on emotion, but on His enduring presence in word and sacrament. Jesus did not promise that the born-again would never sin. He promised that He would not abandon them. "I am with you always, even to the end of the age" (Mt 28:20).

Chapter 6

Recovering the Whole Story

The story, and what Jesus means to be "born again," began neither in a revival tent nor in a single emotional moment or self-declaration. It started with Jesus Christ, standing before Nicodemus under the cover of night, revealing the mystery of *new life from above*. This life begins in water and Spirit and unfolds over a lifetime. Long before Christ's public ministry, Scripture had already prepared the ground for this mystery through God's repeated use of water and Spirit as instruments of cleansing, rebirth, and re-creation. What Christ does is not invent something new but fulfill and sacra-mentalize what God had been revealing all along.

Throughout Christian history, the phrase "born again" has journeyed from the heart of Jesus's teaching to the center of modern religious iden-tity. Not once does Scripture teach the modern formula of "accepting Jesus into your heart" or "praying the sinner's prayer." As Steve Ray notes, these phrases are not in the Bible at all. What *is* in the Bible is the consistent language of water, Spirit, washing, rebirth, and incorporation into Christ through baptism. The Apostles never separated faith from baptism. When Peter preached at Pentecost, the people asked, "What must we do?" and he answered: "Repent and be baptized every one of you in the name of Jesus Christ for the forgiveness of your sins, and you will receive the gift of the Holy Spirit" (Acts 2:38).

Once conversion is framed primarily as a decisive inner moment, renewal itself must be repeatedly re-created through new moments of intensity. The Christian life becomes dependent on remembered experiences and renewed emotional urgency. Historic Christianity approaches renewal differently. When faith cools, or sin intervenes, the path back is not the manufacturing of another crisis but repentance and grace. In the Catholic Church, this ordinary return takes concrete form in the sacrament of reconciliation (confession)—repentance, absolution, and the grace of Christ into the life first given in baptism, restoring communion rather than replacing it. Confession is not a denial of being born again; it is the fruit of it.

For the "born again" Christian, falling into sin often becomes deeply disruptive, not only morally but existentially. Depending on the preacher one follows, the answers can be conflicting and destabilizing. Some, such as Ray Comfort, suggest that if a person "dives into sin," they were never truly born again in the first place—perhaps they may *fall* into sin, but never dive into it.[13] In the end, this language exposes the instability of the system itself: *Did I fall, did I dive, or did I jump?* No one can say with certainty, because subjective self-assessment almost always minimizes culpability or exaggerates despair, leaving the believer trapped in ambiguity rather than restored by grace. A framework that requires believers to parse whether they "fell," "dived," or "jumped" into sin ultimately replaces repentance with self-analysis, substituting uncertainty for the objective mercy Christ entrusted to His Church.

Others acknowledge that genuine believers do sin after conversion yet offer differing explanations and remedies. Many simply advise asking God for forgiveness, but without any objective means of restoration, assurance remains largely subjective. By contrast, the Church offers a cohesive, logical, and sacramental path for renewal, one instituted by Christ Himself, through which grace is restored, communion is healed, and the believer is strengthened to begin again.

---

13 Comfort, "True and False Conversion.".

This book has traced that journey—beginning with Christ's conversation with Nicodemus, through the sacramental life of the early Church, and onward to the revivalist movements and contemporary Evangelical culture. At each stage, the meaning of new birth has shifted, sometimes deepening, sometimes narrowing, but always reflecting the spiritual hunger of those seeking renewal.

At its source, Jesus's words, "Unless one is born of water and the Spirit, he cannot enter the kingdom of God," point directly to baptism as the beginning of Christian life. The earliest Christians understood this rebirth not as a fleeting emotional experience, but as a lifelong transformation initiated by God's grace. Baptism was the doorway, catechesis the preparation, and ongoing conversion the journey. The sacraments, the community of faith, and daily discipleship all worked together to nurture this new life.

Over time, however, the language of "born again" became increasingly associated with personal decision and emotional assurance. Revivalist preaching and modern Evangelicalism emphasized the moment of conversion, sometimes at the expense of the sacramental and communal dimensions of faith. While these movements awakened many to the reality of grace, they also risked reducing the mystery of rebirth to a formula or a feeling.

Yet the whole story of grace is far richer. Grace is not merely a feeling or a one-time event—it is the divine life of God dwelling in the soul, transforming and sustaining us through every season. Biblically, grace is not merely God "being nice" or overlooking faults. It is God's active, effective gift that *does something* in the person—rescues, strengthens, transforms, and sustains. Paul says we are "justified freely by his grace" (Rom 3:24), and that salvation is "by grace … not your own doing" (Eph 2:8). But grace is also power: "My grace is sufficient for you, for my power is made perfect in weakness" (2 Cor 12:9). It trains and reforms the soul: "The grace of God … trains us to renounce ungodliness … and to live upright" (Ti 2:11-12). In Scripture, grace isn't only pardon; it is divine life at work—God enabling what we cannot do by nature, bringing real inward renewal.

Baptism plants this grace within us; the sacraments nourish it; conversion renews it. The Christian life is not a static status, but a dynamic journey—a daily invitation to be remade in the image of Christ. The Church, called *Mater Ecclesia*, the Mother of the Reborn, reminds us that no Christian is born again apart from the Body of Christ. To separate rebirth from the Church is to separate it from the source of divine life itself. Jesus established a living community, not a collection of isolated individuals.

Through the Church, the Spirit continues to give life, and through the sacraments, grace is continually renewed. As St. Cyprian of Carthage (third century) put it: "He cannot have God as Father who does not have the Church as Mother" (*On the Unity of the Church* 6).

To reclaim the language of rebirth is to embrace both the decision to follow Christ and the sacramental reality of baptism. It is to recognize that being "born again" is not a single moment to be remembered, but a lifelong adventure of grace—a continual participation in Christ's resurrection. The invitation is not simply to ask, "Have you been born again?" but to live the life that was born in you, returning to the font, the faith, and the Church that gave you birth. The invitation of Christ remains unchanged: to be born of water and Spirit, to enter into the lifelong adventure of grace, and to live as members of His Body. The mercy of Christ was never meant to be guessed at—it was meant to be received.

Practical Applications
Living the Whole Story

1. **Rediscover Baptism's Meaning:** Reflect on your baptism—not just as a past event, but as the beginning of your spiritual journey. Consider how it shapes your identity and your relationship with God.

2. **Engage in Lifelong Conversion:** Make repentance, prayer, and growth in virtue regular parts of your life. See conversion not as a one-time crisis, but as a daily turning toward Christ.

3. **Participate in the Sacramental Life:** Attend Mass or worship regularly, receive the sacraments, and let them nourish your faith. Recognize that grace is given and renewed through these visible signs.

4. **Embrace Community:** Connect with your local church or faith community. Share your journey, support others, and allow yourself to be supported. Remember, rebirth happens within the Body of Christ, not in isolation.

5. **Live Out Your Baptism Daily:** Let your actions reflect the new life you have received. Practice charity, forgiveness, and service. Work out your salvation "in fear and trembling," trusting that God is at work within you.

6. **Seek Ongoing Formation:** Continue learning about your faith–through Scripture, study, and spiritual reading. Let your understanding of grace and rebirth deepen over time.

7. **Invite Others into the Whole Story:** Share the fullness of Christian rebirth with others–not just as a moment of decision, but as a lifelong adventure of grace. Encourage those around you to rediscover the richness of baptism, sacrament, and community.

May we answer Christ's invitation anew, living the whole story of grace, and becoming ever more fully the people God calls us to be.

A Prayer

Lord Jesus Christ, You do not leave us to search for You in uncertainty,

but come to us through water, word, and bread. Teach us to meet You where You promised to be in the mercy of confession, in the life of baptism, and in the gift of Your Body and Blood.

Make our relationship with You not merely remembered, but lived and renewed each day by Your grace, until we dwell with You forever.

Thank You

Before closing, I want to offer a few words of gratitude.

First, to my friend Tom, whose encouragement prompted me to reconsider my faith and begin seeking Christ more seriously. To my parents, who first handed on the Catholic faith – a foundation I only later understood as a living gift. And above all, to the grace of God, who patiently led me beyond confusion and into the discovery that a personal relationship with Jesus is not something we construct within ourselves, but something He gives to us – concretely, faithfully, and repeatedly – through the sacraments He established. There I found not a distant Savior to be imagined, but a present Lord who acts, forgives, nourishes, and remains.

Common Objections

The Thief on the Cross

Those objecting to the need for baptism, and the fact that it is a sacrament of salvation, often appeal to the thief on the cross. Since Christ promised him, "Today you will be with me in Paradise" (Lk 23:43), and since the thief was seemingly not baptized, it is argued that baptism cannot be necessary for salvation. From this, some conclude that faith alone, apart from baptism, is sufficient and that baptism is therefore optional or merely symbolic.

Response Exceptions Do Not Void The Rule

This objection fails on several theological and scriptural grounds. First, Scripture is silent on whether the thief had or had not been baptized. Arguments built on silence cannot establish doctrine. The Gospel text does not present the thief as a counterexample to baptism; it simply records Christ's merciful promise.

Second, and more importantly, the thief's salvation occurs before the institution of Christian baptism as a sacrament of the New Covenant. Christian baptism, as commanded by Christ ("Go therefore and make disciples … baptizing them" [Mt 28:19]), belongs to the post-resurrection and Pentecostal Church. The thief dies under the old covenant, saved directly by Christ's sovereign authority, just as Christ forgave sins during His earthly ministry apart from sacramental rites (see Mk 2:5-10).

Third, even if the thief were unbaptized, this would demonstrate only that God is free to save outside the sacraments, not that the sacraments are unnecessary. Catholic theology has always affirmed this distinction. As St. Augustine explains, "God has bound salvation to the sacrament, but He Himself is not bound by the sacrament" (*On Baptism, Against the Donatists* 4.22). Extraordinary cases do not nullify the ordinary means established by Christ.

Scripture consistently presents baptism as the normative means of entry into the New Covenant:

- "Unless one is born of water and the Spirit, he cannot enter the kingdom of God" (Jn 3:5)

- "Repent and be baptized ... for the forgiveness of your sins" (Acts 2:38)
- "Baptism ... now saves you" (1 Pt 3:21)
- "All of us who have been baptized into Christ Jesus were baptized into his death" (Rom 6:3)

The early Church understood these passages literally and sacramentally. St. Cyprian of Carthage taught unequivocally, "No one can have God as Father who does not have the Church as Mother" (*On the Unity of the Church* 6), grounding salvation within the sacramental life of the Church. St. Ambrose, preaching on baptism, declared, "The water does not cleanse without the Spirit" (*On the Mysteries* 4.20), affirming baptism as the divinely appointed means of regeneration.

The thief on the cross, therefore, represents an extraordinary act of mercy, not a doctrinal template. To elevate an exception into a rule is to misread both Scripture and grace. The Church has never claimed that God cannot save apart from baptism; she has consistently taught that Christ revealed baptism as the ordinary, commanded, and promised means by which new birth occurs. Salvation is God's gift—but baptism is the way He ordinarily gives it.

Salvation Is by Faith Alone, Not by Baptism

Another common objection argues that baptism cannot be necessary for salvation because Scripture teaches that we are saved by faith alone. Passages such as "By grace you have been saved through faith ... not of works" (Eph 2:8-9) are cited to suggest that baptism, being an outward act, would constitute a human work that undermines the gratuity of grace. From this perspective, baptism may serve as a public testimony of faith, but it cannot be a means by which salvation is actually given.

Response: Baptism Is Not a Human Work but God's Work

This objection rests on a false premise: that baptism is a human work performed for God rather than a divine act performed by God. Scripture never treats baptism as a work of the believer earning salvation; it presents baptism as the instrument through which God applies His saving grace.

St. Paul explicitly distinguishes baptism from works of the law when he teaches that God "saved us, not because of works done by us in righteousness, but according to his mercy, by the washing of regeneration and renewal of the Holy Spirit" (Ti 3:5). The phrase "washing of regeneration" is universally recognized by the early Church as a reference to baptism. Far from contradicting grace, baptism Is described as its vehicle.

Likewise, when Paul speaks of salvation by faith apart from works, he is rejecting reliance on human achievement, not denying the means Christ Himself instituted. Faith and baptism are never opposed in the New Testament. On the contrary, they are consistently joined: "He who believes and is baptized will be saved" (Mk 16:16). Faith is the disposition by which baptism is received fruitfully; baptism is the moment at which faith encounters God's saving action.

The Fathers understood this clearly. St. Augustine writes, "When the sacrament of baptism is given, God works invisibly within it" (*Tractates on the Gospel of John* 80.3). St. Gregory of Nazianzus likewise teaches, "Baptism is God's most beautiful and magnificent gift ... the grace of illumination" (*Oration* 40). For the early Church, baptism was not a human offering to God but God's gift to humanity.

Thus, salvation by grace through faith does not exclude baptism; it presupposes it. Baptism is not opposed to grace because it is not a work of man. It is the moment when God acts—cleansing, regenerating, and incorporating the believer into Christ. To reject baptism as "works" is therefore not to defend grace, but to misunderstand how grace is given.

Baptism Is Only a Symbol

It is often claimed that baptism is merely an outward symbol of an inward faith—that the water signifies a salvation already accomplished, rather than effecting anything in itself. From this perspective, baptism is understood as a public testimony of belief, valuable as a witness but unnecessary for regeneration or salvation.

Response: Scripture Presents Baptism as Effective, Not Merely Symbolic

While baptism certainly signifies faith, Scripture does not present it as *only* a symbol. Instead, Scripture consistently attributes real effects to baptism. St. Peter does not say that baptism symbolizes salvation; he states plainly, "Baptism … now saves you" (1 Pt 3:21). Likewise, St. Paul teaches that, through baptism, believers are united to Christ's death and resurrection: "We were buried therefore with him by baptism into death" (Rom 6:4). Such language exceeds mere symbolism and describes participation in a real spiritual event.

The early Church understood baptism as an instrument through which God acts, not a human sign pointing backward to an accomplished salvation. St. Cyril of Jerusalem writes, "You go down dead in sins, and you come up alive in righteousness" (*Catechetical Lectures* 2.4). St. Ambrose similarly affirms, "The water does not heal without the Spirit" (*On the Mysteries* 4.20). For the Fathers, baptism was symbolic precisely because it was sacramental—a visible sign that actually accomplishes what it signifies.

Infant Baptism Is Unbiblical

Another objection argues that baptism requires personal repentance and conscious faith, making infant baptism invalid or unscriptural. Since infants cannot profess belief, it is claimed that baptizing them contradicts the New Testament pattern.

Response: Infant Baptism Flows from Covenant and Apostolic Practice

Scripture nowhere restricts baptism to adults, nor does it require a verbal profession as a prerequisite. On the contrary, baptism is repeatedly described as entry into a covenantal community. St. Peter declares, "The promise is for you and for your children" (Acts 2:39). In the New Testament, entire households are baptized (Acts 16:15, 16:33; 1 Cor 1:16), with no indication that children were excluded.

The early Church unanimously baptized infants, not as an innovation, but as a continuation of God's covenantal pattern. St. Irenaeus writes that Christ

67

came to save "all who through Him are reborn unto God—infants, children, youths, and old men" (*Against Heresies* 2.22.4). St. Augustine appeals to universal apostolic tradition: "The custom of baptizing infants is not to be scorned … nor is it to be believed that its tradition is anything except apostolic" (*On the Literal Interpretation of Genesis* 10.23).

Infant baptism affirms that salvation is God's initiative, not the product of human maturity or intellectual assent. Faith is required—but in the Church, faith is first received as a gift before it is later confessed with understanding.

The Spirit Saves, Not Water

Some argue that Scripture teaches salvation by the Holy Spirit alone, rendering water baptism unnecessary. Passages emphasizing the Spirit's role in regeneration are cited to suggest that water is incidental or symbolic at best.

Response: The Spirit Works Through the Water

This objection creates a false opposition between Spirit and sacrament that Scripture itself does not make. Jesus explicitly unites the two when He declares, "Unless one is born of water and the Spirit, he cannot enter the kingdom of God" (Jn 3:5). The New Testament consistently presents water and

Spirit as working together, not in competition.

St. Paul echoes this unity when he speaks of "the washing of regeneration and renewal of the Holy Spirit" (Ti 3:5). The Spirit is the agent; baptism is the means. St. Basil the Great explains, "The Spirit is given in baptism, but the water prepares the way" (*On the Holy Spirit* 15.35). Likewise, St. Augustine famously taught, "Take away the word, and what is the water but water? Add the word, and it becomes a sacrament" (*Tractates on John* 80.3).

To affirm that the Spirit saves is entirely correct. But Scripture and tradition insist that the Spirit ordinarily saves through the means Christ appointed. Water baptism is not a rival to the Spirit; it is the instrument the Spirit uses to bring about new birth. When we step back and consider the whole witness of the Christian faith, including Jesus's words to Nicodemus in John 3, the consistent teaching of the apostles, the lived practice of the early Church, and the testimony of Scripture read as a unified whole, a clear and coherent picture emerges. Baptism was never meant to compete with faith or replace the work of the Spirit; it was the ordinary way God chose to give both.

From the beginning, Christians did not ask whether baptism was merely symbolic or strictly necessary in an abstract sense. They simply obeyed

Christ, trusting that He meant what He said when He joined new birth to water and the Spirit. The Church has always recognized that God is free to act beyond the sacraments, yet she has also faithfully taught that He revealed a normal path by which grace is given and life in Christ begins. Read in this light, baptism is not a burden or a technical requirement, but a gift—a concrete moment where God meets the believer, grants new life, and begins the lifelong work of transformation that leads us home.

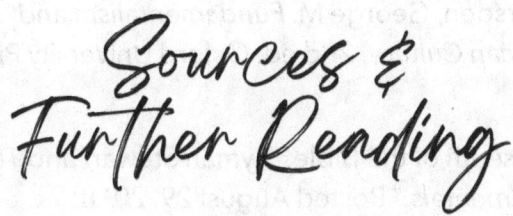
Sources & Further Reading

Ahlstrom, Sydney E. *A Religious History of the American People*. Yale University Press, 1972.

Biola University Archives. "History of *The Fundamentals*."

Bird, Chad. *Upside-Down Spirituality: The 9 Essential Failures of a Faithful Life*. Baker Books, 2019.

Carpenter, Joel A. *Revive Us Again: The Reawakening of American Fundamentalism*. Oxford University Press, 1997.

Colson, Charles W. *Born Again*. Chosen Books / Fleming H. Revell Company, 1976.

Comfort, Ray. "True and False Conversion." Posted August 9, 2019. *https://www.livingwaters.com/true-and-false-conversion/*.

Comfort, Ray. *The Way of the Master*. Living Waters, 2006.

Marsden, George M. *Fundamentalism and American Culture*. 2nd ed. Oxford University Press, 2006.

Museum of the Bible. "Lyman Stewart and *The Fundamentals*." Posted August 29, 2018. *https://www.museumofthebible.org*.

Orthodox Church in America. "Protestant Fundamentalism and Protestant Liberalism." n.d. *https://www.oca.org/orthodoxy/the-orthodox-faith/church-history/twentieth-century/protestant-fundamentalism-and-protestant-liberalism*.

Ott, Ludwig. *Fundamentals of Catholic Dogma*. Edited by James Canon Bastible. Translated by Patrick Lynch. TAN Books, 1974.

Pew Research Center. *Measuring Religion in Pew Research Center Surveys*. Pew Research Center, 2016. *https://www.pewresearch.org/religion/2016/04/19/measuring-religion-in-pew-research-center-surveys/*.

Pietsch, Brian. "The Fundamentals and Their Place in American Religious History." *Fides et Historia* 26, no. 3 (1994): 5–24.

Pitre, Brant. *Jesus and the Jewish Roots of Baptism*. Lecture, St. Paul Center for Biblical Theology, circa 2008–2014.

Ray, Steve. "Are You Born Again by 'Water and the Spirit'?" *Defenders of the Catholic Faith (CatholicConvert.com)*. n.d. *https://catholicconvert.com/further-thoughts-on-water-and-the-spirit/*.

Rood, Paul. "The Stewart Brothers, Union Oil, and *The Fundamentals*." Biola University Archives, 2009.

Sandeen, Ernest R. *The Roots of Fundamentalism*. University of Chicago Press, 1970.

Testimony Publishing Company. *The Fundamentals: A Testimony to the Truth*. Testimony Publishing Company, 1910. *https://archive.org/details/fundamentalstest17chic/mode/2up*.

Wright, N. T. *John for Everyone: Part One*. Westminster John Knox Press, 2004.